SACRED SOUL

**SVETLA
YORDANOVA**

Printed in the United States of America

ISBN 979-8-89114-059-2 (sc)
ISBN 979-8-89114-060-8 (e)

Library of Congress Control Number: 2024901549

2025.03.11

MainSpring Books
5901 W. Century Blvd
Suite 750
Los Angeles, CA, US, 90045

www.mainspringbooks.com

CONTENTS

TOUCH

There are moments when
something touches you,
which changes your life:
a fortuitous shadow of a bird
swiftly fused with yours;
a rain-drop.
which had the courage to fight your tears;
the Morse code of a woodpecker,
reminding you of the doors
you used to knock at...
And though painful,
this thing unlocks your heart
and opens your soul to the memory.

You can probably guess,
that the bread might tell
something more about itself,
when the knife touches it...

UNTITLED

> The world is so huge
> many-sided
> it needs something
> other than interpretation"
> Ana Blandiana

You could forget.
Everything.
That effort would be nothing else,
but silence with another name.
Absurdity, and sometimes rapture
is this wounded life
a painting in the thoughts,
a dream which lost its sacred content.
And it could be something more...

Your consciousness of life is elusive,
unpredictable, like the prayers of anyone
who bears in his heart Expectation.

Such a pity, so strange.
that your name might be sorrow,
passion, forgotten by a caustic word,
victory over your reckless perseverance.
From your point of view
you recognize only your pains,
and they are the injured lapses
remaining without a memory in your past.
You re-create them
on the sheet of white paper
with help from the fever
of the truth of life,

which alone is reality
that doesn't have a permanent home.

ICARUS SOLILOQUY

If it happens
that I'm to blame for something,
I don't want anthropoids for confession.
I'll look for birds
to confess to them
my Despair.
I'll ask them to pardon me
for my audacity...

If I die,
don't give me to the worms
don't gash a wound in the earth.
It's not the soil's fault that I had lived...

Leave my body to the birds beaks
after a time
look for me in a bird.

Icarus- in Greek mythology, the son of Daedalus,
who with his father, escaped from the labyrinth in
Crete, using wings made from feathers,
fastened with wax. Icarus plunged to his death when he
flew too near the Sun, and the wax melted.

THE SEVENTH DAY

Of all human qualities,
Astonishment within us is most in excess.
Without it,
the wonders of the world
are bizarre formations,
untouched by vanity and lust.

Silence suits the valued things.
The valued things live
in the solitude of the Moment
a seed, conscious of eternity.

At midday Sunday
useless conversations
a kaleidoscopic mosaic in Gossip's dream.
And the peace is something more...

The hour after dinner is full of thoughts,
intrusive, like Greed's success.
Old women gossiping,
with assured, yet powerless, self-will.

And in the screech of a bird
nailed into the fleshy flank of the night;
in the bright pupil of a child;
in the silence of the poet
vulnerable temptation to the words,

the Astonishment is always in excess...
And it is a conception of imagination,
which
can deform things.

HUMAN QUESTIONS

There is no distinguishing mark
save the cross with inscription.
And even the name
can be repeated.

How could you prove
that you existed,
since the heirs themselves
forget each other,
much less remember you?

How could you prove
that this land too provided you wheat,
since your star
falls down, pierced by
the decision of destiny?
How could you distinguish yourself
from the multitude of humans,
in order that only a chosen group
remembers you?
We are all one and the same thing

we were born,
                we lived,
                                we created
and we died at the sunset of our lives!

LIKE HIPATIA·

If I prefer the rage of the wind,
That's only to avoid overhearing
the senseless reproaches and words,
with which my views are denounced...

Now I await them
without fear or guilt,
to reassure myself.
that they we're lost long ago
outside the truth of my Museuma.

I know someone's black hands
will take away my life,
with sticks and stones,
and probably torture in
the city square too,
but never again do I want to be shielded.

My wisdom wants me strong-
"the truth doesn't need a guardian."

… Hipatia -- /380 - 415/ - daughter of Teon, a famous mathematician
and astronomer at the end of the four, century. She devoted herself
to the secrets of astronomy and philosophy. She died as a martyr
on Konoriyu Square in Alexandria. Alexandria was also the site,
the Museuma- a portal to world knowledge. It was giant structure
with marble columns, housing a cultural center with an enormous
library, parks, and gardens.

GOOD IS CONSCIOUSNESS

I can scare you ...
Without blowing through the branches
of knitted, painful conversations;
but the wind is vulnerable too.
I can hiss...
Without sleeping long
under the stone of Indifference;
because there is something between
selflessness and hatred.
I can yell in despair and bite...
Without being chased by a small beast,
seen before in children's books;
or by a man, who grew into a monster.
I can rob and kill...
Without being granted something;
a desired meeting with the good hearts,
because there are such indeed...

I sense why GOD
introduces us to animals in our lifetime
predators, reptiles, ungulates...
Probably
to be left with the feeling,
that we contain a piece of each of them.
And if He manages to gain a victory
over us,
that's because of the guilt we feel
when we kill an animal
or transform ourselves into one.

PHILOSOPHY

I wonder if,
when you get insulted
or when someone always disturbs
your useful reviving silence,
it is all the same
to the birth of the Change,
which will give shelter to the doubts.

I wonder if,
you will remain good now,
when each day begins
with thoughts of the daily bread
or after the distrust-shown towards you,
it is all the same
to your pure virtues.

Probably it depends on the person...

There is something common and definite-
fresh or stale
the bread is with equal price.

LOCKSMITH

The fire of the gossip
turned his life into ash.
He lived with his-tragedy for a long
time,
until the pardons abandoned his heart
and the solitude turned him into a
stone.

In order not to die from starvation
he started to make keys
so people could enter their homes,
and keep their vanity locked in.

But he didn't want a key
to his own door
he always kept thinking,
that if he sticks
the key in the keyhole,
he might remove
someone's prying eye.

DREAM

The town, hurt by words,
resounded with screams
the people, gathered,
stormed the city square.
No culprits nor defeated.
The only concern,
roaming anxiously in my conscience
was born in the thought:
if only the monument
survives the offending shouts.
I was reaching out my hands,
breathlessly wriggling
my body through the crowd,
hurt from rough shoulders
struggling quickly to reach the marble...
But somehow I failed to get through
two agile children, with weepy eyes
propelled by the crowd,
disturbed the sun with a small banner:
"WE TOO WANT...EXPANSE,
SKY...THINK ABOUT US!"

I suddenly awoke.
The day was holding a flag
It was not on its knees,
asking the night for forgiveness...
Today I will believe in birds,
and tomorrow
in my son
and I will fearlessly think
about the strike of the conscience!

THE VISIONARY

He was a very good man.
But he had an accident
he went blind,
suddenly and irreparably.

In time, his hearing sharpened.
He could even sense
the little spider delicately
touching its web!

But his destiny changed -
he was rewarded with a selfless girl,
kissing him on the forehead.
And there
in the course of kissing,
appeared a dimple...

It was
the third eye
of the visionary.

SOMETHING MORE

To my son - Bozhidar

The day of my rescuing
consolation for the tiredness
with honor to the quiet doom.

The appearance in front of this path
obscuring, absorbing
and yet renewing the view in front of me.

And I am the same
the words are still signs,
which I use while
for the sensual confession ...

In the eyes of this love and God
I am something more
than Femininity
creator of a soul.
but incompatible, like grand piano and
silence,
with the present-day world under the Sun.

CLOSE TO GOD

For Z.K.

Multifaceted is your entity!
To doubt everything
which is ostensibly complete...
To let every fragment of you
accept the things,
running away from your discord.
To be naive each time you fall in love
until you truly believe,
that real Love is a door
for which you don't have a key.
And to still hope!
To look for the invisible
with clear image only in your dreams.
To move ahead
dreaming for additional senses
to help see
the panoramic view of your Path.

In order to regulate precisely
the scales of life
whether you are closer to God
or to the others
who are blind to you
Your entity is
in the bifurcations
of the Soul.

CHOICE

He was punished.
The man who. all his life,
lived for others.
And yet he was pitied
he was given the opportunity to choose:
either to sever his arms
or to deprive him his legs.

The choice was difficult for him.
He lived a full and useful life.
He walked great distances
looking for the right way.
That is why he chose
to do without his legs...

From now on,
he would need the arms
to embrace more!

AN INTERESTING TWIST

After our death SOMEONE is happy.

The death itself
because of its victory over us.
The soul
because of its freedom.
The sky
which becomes lighter without a star.
And the surviving friends
who pretend to mourn us,
but in their grief
hide one of their faces.
And the soil is happy
it has so many children to feed...

Only Life will cry,
for it knows the reason.

MISSION

A sheep had to be slaughtered.
Three people were- chosen to do this
a doctor, a beggar and a poet.
Courage showed the beggar in his
hunger...
Having entered into a treaty with the
knife,
Death hovered over the miserable
animal.

And preoccupied by the slaughtering,
they didn't notice the face of the poet
he was looking at its heart woefully.
Suddenly, he felt a waft over himself
the soul of the sheep was around
and it seemed it had whispered something...
The Soul of the sheep chose him
to take its aborted lamb he, the poet.
would place it in the grave.

HOSPITAL

I'm lying on the bed
in a white room
with a young guest in my body
disease incessant in its rage

Upstairs- birth is given,
Downstairs- the morgue.
And I - in the middle between puerperal yell
and deathlike silence.

With the hope of recovering
I am finding strength within myself to
think,
whether the Disease
is a warning of Life
or a right hand of Death?

BURDEN

I had an opinion of myself,
to which I no longer conform.
The world draws up trajectories,
and the risk falls in love
with its memories.
And there is not a chance to return
to my blissful, merry naivete.
The path in front of me does not
surprise me,
I am standing there, hoping to discover
simply the arms of the Secret...
And I am full of life, ambitions and
silence
so necessary for the proper view
of my Soul.
I've turned my back on Meekness
and I laugh at the pains
with the symbolic red thread
which wards off evil.

I am full of life!
The body splits into two
part of me is sending signals
with tender pulsation and sleeplessness!

The world draws up trajectories,
and the risk swelled up inside me.

MOTHERHOOD

I will walk through you with flair...
Like in a room with a multi-eyed carpet
I will enter your presence.
Because now
the Motion will start from within me.
My blood is ready
for this most-womanly initiation.
I understood from my shouts while
sleeping,'
from the thrill reposed within me.
And I am breathing
with the burden
of my new sensuality.
Which will continue in another body.

And this small body
is my freedom,
borrowed.

MERCY

If we judge people
by the temper of their watch-dog,
we would know nothing
about the hatred and the envy.
And for the rose-colored glasses too!

A surprise is every motion.
That's why the birds are not accustomed
to
the handful of crumbs from the good-hearted.

When we would enter the orphanage
with veneration and faith,
with which we light candles in the
temple;
when the flocks would set off alone
without a shepherd;
when the peace would not dream bullets
and a child alone would think
of a fairy-tale about the womb,
then
we will be worthy of the Sun...
And true friends of the dogs!

GREEN MELODY

When the stillness
does not stake its soul
on someone's vigilant silence,
but dreams of footprints;
when the trees
reach out their green-cupped hands
for the song of the birds;
when before sunset
something stirs the air
the breathing of the oarsman,
who all through the winter
dreamed of a river;
when the lovers rush into the forest
to awaken the shadows -

then the night
is no longer its own master...

DINNER WITH TEARS

At the place where it all happened,
between the sin and the accusations,
the day turned its back on fate
and went after its weary sun
to go to its bed in the west.

What's left was the moan
and the taste of the beating
as a halo
around the twisted body.
And there is no way in your heart,
to feel another's misfortune,
because the wail and the tears
are the pinnacle of Despair,
which evoked your greatest human
horror.
But perhaps love is to blame,
when it is hurt by time?
You are standing.
And only the sticky words -
in the middle of the crowd
are prompting you,
to keep silent.
It is the best for the time being...
Until you comprehend why,
the woman,
beaten by her husband,
wishes not to tell.

A TALE FOR THE PAIN

The Pain was taking a
walk alone along the
street content with
herself that she freed
one heart,
which burst suddenly.

Now she continues her march
with the desire to maintain her identity.
But the ones whom she met with
were already immune to sufferings...

The Pain didn't find a
way to their hearts.
She remained on the street by a stone,
which asked her to give him life.

DOUBLE-FACE

One face of this house
is ivy-green
with the trellised vine in front
to feed the boisterous grandchildren.

The second is the scandals,
when the silence goes away...

Double-faced is this house.
Nest of ghosts, whose bodies
were bored to death...

BODY

Every morning
in the warm place
where he had slept,
he always saw traces of
some letters.
He started to get used to them.
He was always waiting impatiently
to finish his dream,
in order to see them again
a long alphabet now...

Thus he understood,
that his body
was composing something
which slowly detached itself
from the soul.

RISK AND POWER

The risk remains!
But is it power,
doubled philanthropy or predominance
over oneself and the vanity?
One suffers and lives
with faith out of love.
One learns to love out of love.
To keep the spirit alive,
hopes, tired from running,
arc preserved again with love.

Risk and power- it's all the same,
when you are a shelter
for harmonic worlds,
which save you...
for the life of the past memories,
for the ambivalence at present,
for the pains of the future.
Because you will endure them too.
For them you are always prepared.
Your spirit is a fire,
and it is needed for the best light
to remain in one heart...

Then risk is born from power!

HEARTACHE

I wouldn't have loved you like I do,
if it wasn't for this sadness,
rooted deeply between us.
I wouldn't have been a haven for
secrets -
a painting with its meaning
hidden from others!
There wouldn't have been time
to relive the hours
when excited and naked,
our kisses kindled the fire of passion.

There wouldn't have been a chance to
grasp Happiness
a tiny piece of soap
you thought you had lost
in the River of Life.
And I, anxiously awaiting again
our next meetings,
only now understand:
Only if you are cold during the winter,
will you sense
the approaching footsteps of Spring.

SPRING

In this hour of the morn,
when over the green leaf
of the land
the day rhymes sun with smile,
my tenderness lifts up
over the light green of the branches,
to partake of the laugh
of the early-rising birds.

And totally like me
these flower gardens are
warm and tender!
I don't know why my love
springs out of me like a brook,
when I touch every tiny blade of grass
with my lively eyes.
If it wasn't I, would someone else
be able to see these melodious moments,
this tiny similarity,
between the little eye of the spring
bird,
and the Earth, ready to give birth.

LIGHT

In the obscurity of the bell
prayers arc tolling,
from lips - sinful and sinless
they find their shelter.
The Feast
smokes the last of an incense pipe
and partakes in the bowl
of sacramental wheat.

The silence gives way to the crucifix
now even the dead forgive the alive.
The candles are stars
on our way to God...

THROUGH A DOG'S EYES

He was strongly attached to dogs.
He was ready to stay hungry
on their behalf.
He couldn't leave them behind
with indifference
he played with them like old friends.

I started to think:
this man in his former life
was most likely a dog
homeless and chased...

Now he looks
through a man's soul
searching for what he missed
in his past life!

LOVE

I'm just one good word
from the poem
you were writing,
when Destiny introduced us.

Since then
you wrote nothing.
But that didn't bother you
you understood,
that each of your thoughts,
gestures, wills, hopes
are the poems
you didn't write on a sheet of paper
but preserved within you forever.

SYNCHRONY

I understand him so well,
that I have the feeling
of fusion.
I understand each of his steps,
gestures and smiles.
His guilt I accept as mine.
I've always been worthy of his presence.
His desires are mine too,
already entrusted
to his knowledge of life.
We are good towards the birds.
Rich with thoughts arc our confidences.
Telepathically disposed
even when we make love...

But if sometimes I get tired
of this identity,
the reason is not that I'm unable
to hide anything from him,
but to look on this synchron
from afar- as if an observer,
who could easily see
any delusions and errors between us...

HERESY

The labyrinth cannot discern
that it gathers the footprints of
searching.
The direction cannot sense,
that it's more needed to the return.
The beauty cannot feel that it exists,
if it cannot compare itself to the ugly.
Wisdom cannot perceive,
that its womb was the solitude.

And you, my darling, will not grasp,
that even if labyrinths shackle my steps;
even if broken in spirit and tired,
I lose my direction
and my beauty throws itself
into someone else's arms,
Wisdom will ripen confidently in me.
As the fateful thought
whatever happens to you,
I will be like a heretic in your absence.

THE SUMMER

The summer is full of words
and the ghostly shadow in the dream
acquires flesh, endowed with full moon.

The summer-exciting infinity,
time for meetings
under the nacreous shine of the stars.

For the woman, who loves
a labyrinth of tender passions.
A discovery of the coziness of
Selflessness.

For the child-long acrobatics
of contemplative discoveries
in the talent of the dreams.

For the old- a perky look
into the pulse of their search for herbs
A hush before the wounds of the
experience.

The summer!
Piano sounding
sunny and sand-bound

The summer!
A thorn in the others seasons' sides.

BEYOND PAIN

Many things beyond Success
are under somebody's power and will.
Vulnerable and fragile they are,
like dandelion fluff.

Many things beyond Happiness
Are under the power of a certain Time:
tired of sharing Selflessness,
which can change the past.

Many things beyond Pain
are under somebody's power and will.
Quietly getting over the sorrow;
and rest which prolonged the memory.
A faint whistle at midnight
caught by the fishing rod
of the sleeplessness.

Beyond The Pain
you arc under the power of another,
a greater one.
And the old, healed wounds
are now an advantage.

BIRD

Of all things. the bird is most
defenseless,
when it's on the ground.
In such moments
the safety gets lost.
But it is in the name of a life.
carried by wings.

In the name of the successful flight.
It is worth the risk to rest awhile
just as the still bird,
on the ground,
gathers strength.

DESTINY

Restless run-
to be persevering is now a sin,
because the Envious punish you.
You temper your legs with labor
and in the evening you write
for the others to think.
And Silence - her escape
nuzzles its face in the vanity
of your satiated hope...

Restless run within yourself
that is your destiny,
you poet.

SACRED SOUL

I will start believing
that someone had wanted to be left
alone
to defend his soul.
and to pursue, though slowly,
the Dream:

I will start believing,
that "even a thought
of someone's presence
is not freedom."
My Solitude
is hurt by Envy.

I will start believing,
because I stopped thinking.
Not to think about anything
is now in itself something-the body rests.
It transforms energies
leads a different life
for the survival of the Soul.

HOMO SAPIENS

We stare with unperceiving eyes,
we hope with trepidation,
we expect helplessly
something new to come.
Since we arc saved- we go.
Since we arc loved- we wait.
Since someone's impudence restrains us
we clutch fists in our empty pocket.
We want to know
whether we will be different,
can we wield power
over the everlasting matter.
The nature castigates us,
and we struggle powerlessly.
And we still believe we can
master it.
We think that we live,
but we just exist
in moments, dreamed up
by Time - The Juggler.

SOMEONE ELSE

Sometimes I feel confused,
when I realize with mysteriousness
and sudden surprise,
that I am not only me,
but at the same time someone else.

But I have gotten used to it
and it doesn't frighten me
I endure both- myself and the other influence...

But I am beginning
to look with a little jealousy
upon my best poems!

PERSPECTIVE

If there was no perspective,
the visible world
would have been more attainable.
net the money would not
have seemed so insufficient...

NOW
Is blessed,
If I exclude the thought
of THEN.

Now is enough for me.
Now I am alive.
I Want nothing.

For the time being...

ABOUT THE AUTHOR

Svetla Yordanova was born on September 2, 1962 in the town of Gorna Oryahovitsa, BULGARIA.

Her first book of poetry "The Spirit of Fire" was published in 1992, and the second - "Sacred Soul" was published in 1995 in a bilingual version - Bulgarian and English.

On August 12, 1996, Svetla received an official copyright certificate for her book " Sacred Soul " at the Library of Congress in Washington.

The following are the books:

- "Choose Your Game" - 1996,
- "Tears in Colorado" - 1999,
- "I think with my heart" - 2001

On April 5, 2005, Svetla won third prize in the National Poetry Competition in Sofia, organized by the "Nikola Y. Vaptsarov" cultural center.

In May 2005, she won a prize in a literary contest organized in her hometown - G. Oryahovitsa.

At the beginning of 2006, the Bulgarian publishing house "Avangard Print" - the city of Ruse, published "The Birthday of the Rain", a book of three stanzas. In the same year, Svetla brought her book "Saved Soul" to the attention of the American publisher in Pittsburgh, who approved it and published it again.

In 2007, Svetla published poems in "A Treasury of American Poets III" - League of American Poets, /p.125/.

In 2009, "Faber" publishing house - Veliko Tarnovo, published her book "Dreams in America".

In 2014, George Hook's collection "BEST HOOKED ON HAIKU" published her works.

In 2023, together with the Bulgarian poet Kancho Velikov, Svetla published a joint book of poetry - lyrics "Star Rivers".

In December 2023, her new book "Shadow to the other shore" - triptych - was published.

In early 2025 Svetla published her next book "Glimpses of the Calendar" - Faber Publishing House V.Tarnovo.